R2003702707

W9-DFC-292

Exploring World History

LATIN AMERICA

Mason Crest
450 Parkway Drive, Suite D
Broomall, PA 19008
www.masoncrest.com

Printed and bound in the United States of America.
First printing

9 8 7 6 5 4 3 2 1

Series ISBN: 978-1-4222-3529-4
ISBN: 978-1-4222-3535-5
ebook ISBN: 978-1-4222-8355-4

Cataloging-in-Publication information from the Library of Congress is
on file with the publisher.

On the Cover: Christianity is the dominant religion in the region—
this statue of Jesus towers over Rio de Janiero, Brazil; the Aztec
civilization once controlled lands in what is now Mexico; Simon
Bolívar led several nations to independence from Spain; the Amazon
River rainforest is home to some of the world's most exotic creatures,
such as this poison dart frog.

Exploring World History
Africa
Australia
China
India
Japan
Latin America
North America
Polar Regions

Contents

An *Aymara woman from Lake Titicaca in Bolivia. She is weaving cloth using a traditional loom tied around her back.*

NORTH AMERICA

ATLANTIC OCEAN

Florida

Gulf of Mexico

Tula

Teotihuacan

Lake Texcoco

Chichen-Itza

BAHAMAS

Tenochtitlan

CUBA

Mount Popocatepetl

YUCATAN

Monte Alban

Palenque

HISPANIOLA

Tikal

JAMAICA

PUERTO RICO

CENTRAL AMERICA

WEST INDIES

Caribbean Sea

TRINIDAD

Isthmus of Panama

Orinoco River

GUIANA HIGHLANDS

Mouths of the Amazon River

Lake Guatavita

Rio Negro River

Río Branco River

Mount Chimborazo

Amazon River

Ucayali River

Amazon Basin

AMAZON RAIN FOREST

Madeira River

SOUTH AMERICA

Cordillera Oriental

Chan Chan

Cajamarca

Machu Picchu

Sacsahuaman

Cuzco

PANTANAL

BRAZILIAN HIGHLANDS

Paracas

Lake Titicaca

MATO GROSSO

Nazca

Potosí

PACIFIC OCEAN

GRAN CHACO

Paraguay River

Atacama Desert

Paraná River

PAMPAS

Patagonia

Río de la Plata Estuary

Cuernos del Paine

Tierra del Fuego

Cape Horn

The landscapes of Latin America vary a great deal. There are high mountains, rain forests and beaches of white sand. If you travel inland to the Brazilian northeast, there is a desert-like region where rivers only flow for a few months of the year.

The puma, many species of monkey, the armadillo, the anteater, the llama, the **alpaca**, snakes, crocodiles, lizards, hummingbirds and parrots are just some of the amazing animals of Latin America.

1 Exploring Latin America

The Story of Latin America

Where is Latin America?

Latin America is in the western hemisphere and has the Atlantic Ocean on its east side and the Pacific Ocean to the west. America is really a double continent made up of both North and South America linked by Central America. The central and southern parts of this continent are called Latin America.

The Countries of Latin America

The name "Latin America" is quite recent. It first came into use in France in around 1860. When we talk about Latin America we think of one North American country (Mexico), the six small **republics** of Central America, three Caribbean countries (Cuba, the Dominican Republic, Haiti) and all of the Spanish-speaking republics of South America as well as Portuguese-speaking Brazil. Surinam and Guyana are not included in Latin America even though they are in South America.

Exploring This Book

This book is divided into seven chapters. This chapter explains the geography of Latin America. The next chapter is an introduction to some of the first people of Latin America and the third chapter looks at the great empires of the Mayas, Aztecs and Incas. The second half of the book (chapters four, five, six and seven) looks at explorers from the fifteenth to the twentieth centuries.

Amerigo Vespucci

How Did Latin America Get its Name?

The first Europeans to settle in Latin America were the Spanish led by Christopher Columbus (1451-1506), an Italian from Genoa. Columbus made other trips to America and brought with him Amerigo Vespucci (1454-1512), an Italian navigator, who wrote about the new land. Amerigo's writings became linked with the area and it was eventually called America, after him.

Latin America also inherits the first part of its name from Italy. The Latins lived in Lazio, the region where Rome was founded. When the Roman Empire became very powerful and conquered almost all of western Europe (first to second centuries), Latin was spoken everywhere. Later on (fifth century), Germanic tribes came from the north of Europe and invaded the Roman Empire, but in Portugal, Spain, France, Romania and Italy, many elements of Roman culture survived. The parts of America that the Spanish and Portuguese explored became known as Latin America.

An Isolated Land

Souh America is an isolated continent. It has many
animals and plants that are found nowhere else on
Earth. During **prehistoric** times it was part of one giant
land mass, called Pangaea. Over millions of years this split
into two smaller land masses, called Laurasia and
Gondwanaland. South America eventually drifted away
from Gondwanaland around 100,000,000 years ago.

The Oldest Coast

The eastern coast of Latin America is **geologically** much
older than that of the west. Although there are mountains
very near the Atlantic Ocean, forming a series of bays and
coves full of small islands, they are not as high as the ones
on the Pacific shore. From the Andes, great rivers run east
into the mighty Amazon River. Another important river,
the Paraná-Paraguay, rises in the heart of the continent and
reaches the sea at the La Plata **Estuary**. Rivers drop from the
mountains in a series of waterfalls and then flow through
fertile plains to the beginning of the **Pampas**.

The Pantanal is a unique region in the middle of the
continent covered with fields and forests which are flooded
for half of the year. These fields are the natural habitat for
rare species of fish, birds and reptiles. It is the world's
largest wetland.

*These are the Eastern Cordillera Mountains of
Bolivia. Cordillera means chain in Spanish.*

*The first people to come to North America crossed
over from Asia via a massive sheet of ice 10,000
years ago. Some moved south to Latin America.*

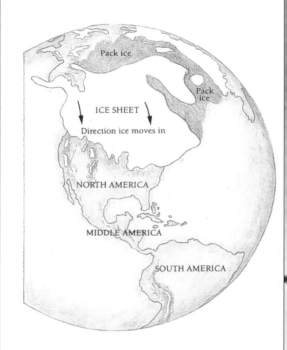

Rain Forests and Mountains

Parts of Latin America are **tropical** and do not have four different seasons like Europe and North America. Along the western coast there are some very high snow-covered mountains which contrast with the almost-constant summer of the rest of the continent. A series of rivers flow east from these mountains to make up some important **fluvial basins**. Among them is the biggest one on Earth—the Amazon Basin.

The Amazon River flows from the west to the east, roughly along the line of the **Equator** to form a great mass of water at the hottest point on the planet. A large part of this water **evaporates** and then falls as rain. This combination of rain and hot weather helped to form the Amazonian rain forest which is full of exotic animals and plants.

Latin America's landscape varies greatly. This is the dramatic Cuemos del Paine mountain in Chile. Cuernos means horn in Spanish.

This is the River Ucayali winding through the Peruvian rain forest. The Ucayali flows into the Amazon, the world's second longest river.

Poison from the skin of the Arrow Poison frog (above) is used by Indians to tip hunting arrows. A jaguar of the Amazon region (below).

2 The Birth of a Culture

Primitive Peoples

The beginnings of human agriculture in Latin America have been found in Ecuador dating from 6600 BCE and in Mexico from 5000 BCE onwards. By c.2000 BCE many thousands of farming villages existed all over Latin America. The people in these settlements hunted rabbits and deer and relied on plants for shelter, clothes, furniture, food, weapons and containers. Potatoes were the main ingredient of any diet and the first people of the Andes managed to breed different types of potatoes to thrive in different types of soil. Eventually, these farmers found a way of freeze-drying food. The potatoes were left outside in the cold all night and then in the sun all day. Every day, the family would walk over the potatoes to squeeze the water out of them. After about a week the potatoes became very light chunks of food that could be stored for up to six years. These dried potatoes were soaked in water before they were eaten.

Modern-day Callaway Indians (from Amarete) harvest potatoes in much the same way as their ancestors did 4,000 years ago.

Some of the places where early human remains have been found in Latin America.

Ancient Latin American people grazed llamas just like these on the Ulla Ulla Plateau in Bolivia.

Wandering Peoples

Many of the first people of Latin America were nomadic—this means that they traveled in small groups from one place to another living on fruit, animals and fish. Some tribes settled, built villages and grew maize (a type of corn), **manioc**, and other roots. People made flour and bread from what they harvested, but they did not have cattle or other animals to help them to farm the land. The only domestic animals they had were the llama, the alpaca, the guinea pig and a kind of tame dog that could not bark.

The First Civilizations

Civilizations first developed in the Central Andes (Peru and Bolivia), Mexico and northern Central America. Hunters and fishermen settled in villages and began farming the land and sea from 2000-1400 BCE. Because the land and sea were very fertile and the inhabitants good farmers and fishermen, the populations of these communities grew very rapidly. Food was easily produced so time became available to develop architecture, religion, cities, armies, pottery and art. The early peoples of Latin America also found time to explore their own country in amazing depth considering all travel was on foot.

What Grows in Latin America?

Many Latin American plants are known world-wide. Corn, tomatoes, potatoes, tobacco, cocoa beans (used for making chocolate and cosmetics) and fruits like pineapples and avocados all came from Latin America. Other **native** plants include manioc, many kinds of **yam** and sweet potatoes, medicinal herbs and a large variety of woods, used both for construction and as sources of dyes for **textile** manufacturers.

A seventeenth-century painting of an Aztec using a digging stick to plant corn (above). An Inca serving dish and maize cobs (below). Maize was made into porridge and tortillas (pancakes) and served with beans.

*T*he main temple of Chavín de Huantar. The Spanish soldiers who came here in the sixteenth century thought that the city had been built by giants.

A map showing the territories of some early northern Andean, Colombian and Exuadorean cultures. Discoveries of some of the earliest remains of pottery, dating from 4000-3000 BCE have been made in modern-day Colombia and Ecuador. The northern Andean cultures are famous for the objects they made out of gold. Other Andean people, such as the Paracas, specialized in depicting complicated stories in cloth.

*T*his is an artist's reconstruction of the Nazca people making their great drawings in the desert.

Influential Cultures

Of all the early cultures of Latin America one of the most fascinating is known as the Chavín. The Chavín were only discovered and explored in 1919 by the Peruvian **archaeologist** Julio Tello. We don't know much about the Chavín except that they built a religious center in a small valley near the village of Chavín de Huantar in Peru. This settlement consists of beautiful temples dating from the height of their power (850-200 BCE). Chavín culture mastered complicated farming and building techniques and made textiles, pottery and objects out of gold. This culture had a great influence on neighboring societies.

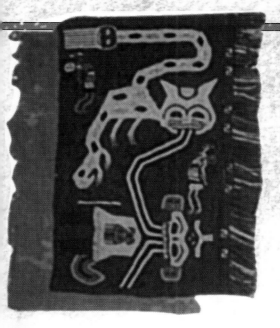

This fragment of Paracas cloth (300-100 BCE) shows a cat god with a long tongue that ends in a human head.

Decorating the Desert

The Paracas (600-200 BCE), also from Peru, were influenced by the Chavín. The Paracas spoke Quechua, which is the second official language of modern-day Peru. From the human remains that have been found we know that these people knew how to perform complicated skull operations. They also made intricate embroideries and beautiful pottery. The Paracas decorated the desert with huge images drawn in the soil which can still be seen today.

The Nazca

Other desert artists include the Nazca (100-1000) of Peru who were also influenced by the Chavín. The Nazca made huge drawings on the ground by removing the dark surface gravel of the earth to reveal the light-colored rock underneath. These pictures of birds and animals can only be seen from the air and we still do not understand their meaning.

The Moche

The culture of the Moche people, in the Moche Valley, thrived for 600 years from the start of the Common Era onwards. The Moche built the Pyramid of the Sun out of mud and straw (called adobe) in the middle of their valley over hundreds of years. This huge pyramid was the largest structure of its kind in Latin America.

The Moche grew enough peppers, peanuts, potatoes and maize on their desert coastline to feed themselves and trade with other peoples inland. Moche artists were very skilled in making pottery, weaving and gold and silversmithing.

A *Pre-Columbian gold mask from Ecuador of a woman with jade eyes.*

The Gold Artists

One of the most advanced people were the Muiscas of (modern-day) Colombia. The Muiscas lived between the Maya people to the north and the Quechua-speakers to the south. The Muiscas were part of the Chibcha-speaking peoples who lived right across Central and South America

The Muiscas built cities out of clay, wood and palms. Their chief, or Bogotá, was adored as if he were a god. Like other Chibcha people in Colombia, such as the **Tairona**, the **Sinu**, the **Quimbaya** and the **Tolima**, they made gold into an amazing variety of beautiful objects, often encrusted with emeralds.

The treasures of the last Bogotá caused his death and the end of the chibcha kingdom. In 1537 the Spanish came looking for gold (see pages 24-33) and the Muiscas were defeated in spite of fierce resistance.

A *gold chest decoration made by the Tolima people of Colombia.*

From the Sea to the Land

The Andean culture of the Chorrera (1200-300 BCE) in Ecuador also had widespread influence. These people abandoned their traditional seafaring way of life and traveled inland to grow maize and manioc. Their society became very prosperous and they developed new techniques for producing pottery.

People Start to Mix

Many Andean societies (especially those in modern-day Peru, Ecuador, Bolivia and Colombia) began to mix and explore each others' cultures because of the trade routes between them. This time, from the sixth to the end of the fifteenth centuries is known as the Integration Period.

The City of Chan Chan

The Chimú people built the great city of Chan Chan on one side of the Moche Valley at the edge of the sea. The Chimú ruled the Lambayeque Valley from about 1350 CE until they were absorbed into the Inca Empire (see pages 21-23) around 1470. Chan Chan consists of about ten large walled mini-cities that cover about 10 square miles. No one really knows how each city functioned but modern-day archaeologists think that when a Chimú ruler died he was sealed up in his city, rather like a huge grave. Another city was then built for the next king.

A *giant stone figure from Highland Bolivia dating from 600.*

This is a ceramic cup bearing the portrait of a ruler of the Moche people of northern Peru (powerful from the first to the seventh centuries).

Early Mexican Cultures

In Mexico and Central America people were not as isolated as in the Andes. Different communities had many things in common, such as large cities, pyramids, a great variety of gods, human sacrifice, a 365-day calendar and hieroglyphs (a type of writing). The peoples of Mexico and Central America also farmed the same type of foods, such as maize, beans, chili and peppers. Instead of many powerful communities existing separately at the same time, as in the Andes, different groups of people rose to power and dominated the others during different stages of history. All the cultures of Mexico and Central America influenced each other at one time or another.

Olmecs and Zapotecs

The Olmecs (1200-400 BCE) came from the shores of the Gulf of Mexico and gradually moved into the highlands. The Olmecs could feed a large population because their farming land was rich and was flooded regularly by surrounding rivers. Their culture produced religious monuments, cave paintings and beautiful sculptures that had a lasting effect on later civilizations.

When the Olmec culture declined, the Zapotecs (800-500 BCE) were one of the largest groups left in the highlands. Their pottery and sculpture were remarkable and they used advanced methods of **irrigation** for farming.

In modern-day Mexico City, theses Toltec statues are reminders of the country's early civilization.

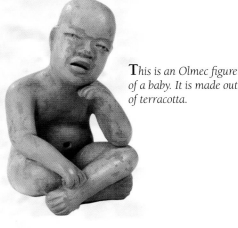

This is an Olmec figure of a baby. It is made out of terracotta.

This massive Olmec sculpture of a ruler from San Lorenzo in Mexico is about 10 feet (3 m) tall.

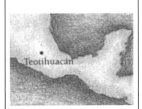

The City of Teotihuacán

Among all the early Mexican peoples, none were more powerful than those who built the city of Teotihuacán in the Valley of Mexico. This civilization dates from the beginning of the Common Era to 600 and had a great influence over the rest of Mexico.

Teotihuacán was probably the capital of a mighty empire, but no written documents have been found relating to it and we know very little about the people who built it. We do know that these people explored the lands to the south and controlled the Maya area (see map on page 15) and that they were successful traders who employed thousands of artists to produce tools and pottery for export to neighboring areas.

The Zapotecs ruled from the city of Monte Albán. Monte Albán is on top of a hill and consists of a huge pyramid surrounded by smaller temples on raised platforms.

This fierce pottery head was found buried with its owner in the city of Teotihuacán.

Worshiping the Sun and the Moon

Teotihuacán was much larger than any city in Europe of the same period. The center of the city covered more than 7 square miles (20 sq km) and was built in a grid pattern. It is thought that the city was inhabited by 125,000-250,000 people in more than 5,000 buildings including at least 2,500 private houses. Teotihuacán had wide streets, temples, tunnels and priests' houses. The two main buildings were pyramids dedicated to the sun and the moon. The pyramids were covered in white plaster and then decorated with brightly-colored mythological scenes. Even after the city's power declined it was of great importance to the Aztecs (see pages 18-20) who made **pilgrimages** to it.

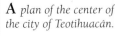

A plan of the center of the city of Teotihuacán.

3 The Great Empires

The Mayas

As Great as the Romans

Many Maya sites were discovered by the American John Lloyd Stephens (1805-52), and the Englishman Frederick Catherwood (1799-1854), on their difficult expeditions through Mexico and Central America from 1839-40 and 1841-42. Catherwood drew many of the cities and **artifacts** that he and Stephens found. The duo's books revealed the huge temples, palaces, weapons and jewels of the Maya civilization. The Mayas ruled at the same time as the Roman Empire in Europe (18 centuries ago). The Mayas were powerful from c.300-900, but by the time the Europeans arrived in Latin America in 1492, their empire had already collapsed because of **civil wars** and invasions by other native groups. The Maya people exist today, but their Empire was succeeded by the Toltecs (see box on page 17) and then the Aztecs (see pages 18-20) who fought the Spaniards in Mexico at the time of the European conquest in the sixteenth century.

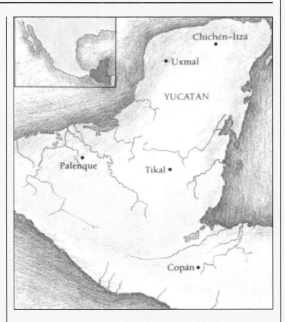

The main cities of the Maya's civilization are shown on the map above. The small boxed map shows the area of Latin America where the Mayas lived.

The Maya temples of Tikal push out of the rain forest of Guatemala. Fifty thousand people lived in houses built on mounds in the 6 square miles around Tikal.

Counting and Writing

Hieroglyphs engraved on monuments prove that the Mayas had an alphabet. We also know that the Mayas had a very accurate system of mathematics which was used to work out complex measurements and **equations**. The Maya calendar was more exact than the European one of the same time, with the year divided into 18 months, each 20 days long. At the end of the year there were five days for celebrations and every four years there was an extra day which made the year a leap year.

This is a drawing of a ball player from a Maya vase (c.500-900 CE). The ball was made of solid rubber and was passed between two opposing teams who were not allowed to touch it with their hands.

A *colored engraving by Catherwood of the temple of Tulum. From* Incidents of Travel in Central America, Chiapas and Yucatán *by Stephens and Catherwood.*

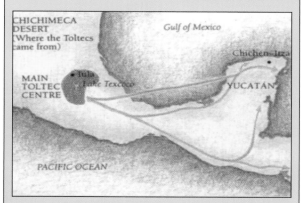

This map shows where the Toltecs originally came from in Central America.

The Maya Temple of the Sun and palace of Palenque in modern-day Mexico.

Cities and Fields

The wealth of the Maya civilization was based on farming, especially maize. The fertile fields made the empire rich and a large population could be fed. The people used their wealth to build cities and create works of art. Some of the cities were surrounded by huge stone walls. Houses were arranged around a large central space where temples and palaces were built. Each Maya city was a state in itself with its own government and laws.

The Toltecs and Chichimecs

From 900 to the time of the Spanish conquest (see pages 24-33) we have much more information about the people of Latin America because archaeologists have learned to read the records these people left behind. We know that the Toltecs (900-1200) came from the north and were hunters and warriors who introduced the bow and arrow to the Maya region. The Toltecs mixed with the Chichimec people and together they founded the city of Tula.

These military statues are in the Toltec capital city of Tula.

The Plumed Serpent

A Maya statue of a man with the head of a jaguar (600-900).

Maize was so important to the Mayas that it was worshiped like a god. Maize had different names depending on whether it was young, sweet or ripe. A snake with feathers, the Plumed Serpent, represented the god that created everything, including maize. The Mayas believed that this serpent had taught people peace. On huge Maya temples and palaces every inch of the stone was decorated in honor of the gods and works of art were created as offerings to the gods.

Around 1200 the Mayas were defeated by the Toltecs from the north. Maya architecture, art and religion was absorbed by the Toltecs and later passed on to the Aztecs.

The Aztecs

Worshiping with Blood

In 1345, the Aztec tribe from the north traveled to the center of Mexico. They founded Tenochtitlán, a large city on a lake, and ruled over the other tribes in the area. The Aztecs were feared and hated warriors, who charged high taxes which made them very rich. The Aztecs believed that the gods had died in order to create the sun and that men should repay the gods with the "sacred water" of human blood.

This wall painting by Diego Rivera (1886-1957) depicts his impression of the building of Tenochtitlán.

This map shows the extent of the Aztec Empire up until 1519. Tlaxcallan and Teotitlan were independent states within the Aztec Empire.

This illustration from the History of the Indies of New Spain *by Diego Duran of 1581 shows Aztecs sacrificing a human being in a religious ceremony.*

This Aztec calendar stone would have been looked after by the priests dedicated to the worship of the sun. The calendar was used for recording religious festivals.

Learning From the Toltecs

In 1440, Emperor Montezuma I improved Tenochtitlán by building **aqueducts** and converting part of the lake into farming land. The wealth and peace of the Aztec Empire attracted Toltec workers and merchants who taught the Aztecs how to make objects out of feathers and gold. The Toltecs also taught the Aztecs how to observe and interpret the stars and how to use a calendar.

The Hero Who Became a God

The god Quetzalcoatl in an Aztec drawing of the sixteenth century.

The Plumed Serpent god of the Mayas and Toltecs was renamed Quetzalcoatl by the Aztecs. In Aztec legend, Quetzal was a hero who was changed into a beautiful bird with long tail feathers who looked like a serpent. The Aztecs believed that this god-hero had been defeated by an evil god and had disappeared with a small group of warriors into the eastern sea. Legend foretold that he would return, at the head of white-skinned, bearded men, to defeat his enemies

Building Islands

According to legend, the Aztecs went in search of a place that had been promised to them by the gods. They had been told to find an eagle sitting on a cactus, holding a snake in its beak (see illustration above). They found the eagle on a rock on an island in the middle of Lake Texcoco and so settled there. The Mexican national flag displays this symbol today. Texcoco was one of five connected lakes in a valley 1.2 miles (2,000 m) above sea level surrounded by volcanoes. Because the island was small, the Aztecs used mud from the bottom of the lake to add more land around the island's edge, but only the land in the center could support stone buildings. The Aztecs built new islands by piling mud onto beds of straw inside wooden fences fixed by stones. As the city grew, channels of water served as streets. The city-dwellers fished in the channels and the lake and grew vegetables on the fertile land of the new islands. Parts of these floating gardens survive today in Mexico City, at Xochimilco.

The turquoise of this two-headed mosaic serpent represents fire.

Aztec Life

It is thought that the Aztec Empire consisted of more than ten million people at its height in the early sixteenth century. Such a large empire needed powerful leadership and warriors became very important in Aztec society. Merchants traveled through the empire trading goods and also acting as spies. A great many documents were written secretly by a special group of priests, rather like a modern-day secret service. The Aztecs wrote these documents in hieroglyphs on paper made out of tree bark. Writing was an important aspect of Aztec life and they wrote lists of taxes, legal documents, religious texts and their own history books.

Trading was a major part of daily life in the Aztec capital of Tenochtitlán. The peoples of the Aztec Empire brought their goods to Tenochtitlán to trade with its 100,000 inhabitants.

The Aztecs exchanged goods and used cocoa seeds as money because they were easy to carry. More than 60,000 Aztecs went shopping in the capital every day. Their markets were well organized but crowded. They could buy everything from food to slaves, pottery, textiles and gold. These markets amazed the Spanish soldiers who came to Mexico at the beginning of the sixteenth century and declared that they had never seen anything to equal them in Europe.

Sacsahuaman is on the outskirts of the modern city of Cuzco and was the scene of many battles.

The Incas

In Ancient times (1500 BCE-1200), there were two main centers of civilization in the Andean region —Nazca, on the Pacific shore and Tiahuanaco, near Lake Titicaca. But around 1100, Quechua-speaking Incas came from the south (Lake Titicaca) to the Andes and founded the city of Cuzco. The Incas eventually started to explore and conquer new lands and finally established the most organized empire of Latin America, which was powerful until c.1530. The Incas built large cities and ruled over a vast territory—the equivalent of modern-day Peru, Ecuador, West Bolivia, North Chile, and northwest Argentina.

The colonial city of Cuzco was built on Inca remains. The **Jesuit** church can be seen in the center.

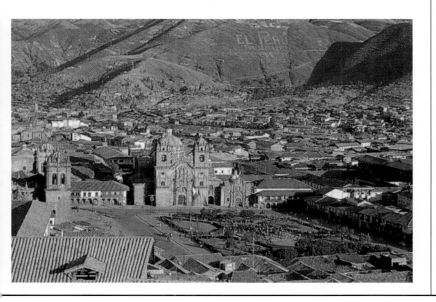

This is a map of the Inca Empire from the time of its first ruler, Manco Capac, who ruled from about 1230, to its final ruler Huayna Capac who ruled from 1493-1525.

A seventeenth-century illustration of the Inca in charge of the quipu.

Writing with Knots

The Incas used a system of strings and knots called *quipu* instead of an alphabet. Several strings hung from a main woolen string and each one was knotted. Each knot, or series of knots, represented a certain event or a quantity. These knots look very complicated to us but the system worked very well for the Incas.

A seventeenth-century drawing of the founder of Cuzco, Manco Capac, the first Inca.

The ruins of the great Inca site of Machu Picchu (below and illustration) were only discovered in 1911. Machu Picchu is only 42 miles (69 km) from the main center of Cuzco but it is remote and situated on a thin mountain ridge 2,050 feet (625 m) above the River Urubamba.

The Child of the Sun

The name "Inca" was originally given to the emperor, who was believed to be the child of the sun. Because the sun was the most powerful Inca god, the emperor (Inca) was a very powerful person. The emblems of the Inca's power were heavy gold discs which hung from his ears and the ears of his family. Family connections were very important in Inca society and each family group formed a clan. Each clan had a leader, but all the clans were controlled by the Inca. The Inca's officials traveled all over the empire to watch over the clans and keep him informed. The Incas built a network of roads that covered the entire empire and yet they didn't have any horses, wheels or carts. All travel across land was on foot. *Tambos* were small buildings dotted along roads at regular intervals. There were probably about a thousand tambos throughout the empire. A messenger ran from one tambo to the next, where another messenger took over—this was how news was conveyed and laws were issued.

Twenty-five thousand miles of roads (like the one below) were built by the Incas.

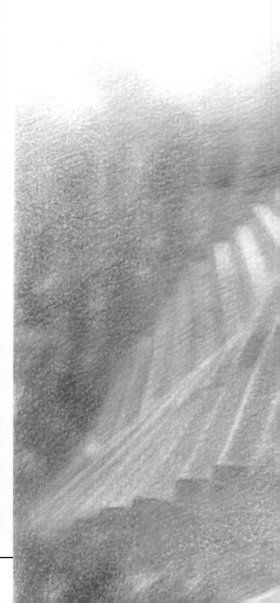

*T*he stones are so tightly fitted together in these original Inca walls (in Cuzco) that it is impossible to slip a sheet of paper between the cracks.

Farmers and Artists

Everybody had to work in Inca society, but no one was paid for the job they did. Children helped to protect the crops by chasing birds away. People built stone terraces on the mountain slopes in order to grow food. Aqueducts and channels carried water to the fields, which were fertilized with the droppings of seabirds. Small animals and food were offered to the sun during religious festivals to please the gods and safeguard the harvest. Huge barns were used to store maize and potatoes, which were divided between the ordinary people, the courtiers and the priests.

Artists were held in such respect that instead of paying taxes their work was given to the people. Skills such as weaving, bronze casting, potting and goldworking were at a very advanced level.

4 The Europeans Arrive

Exploration Fever

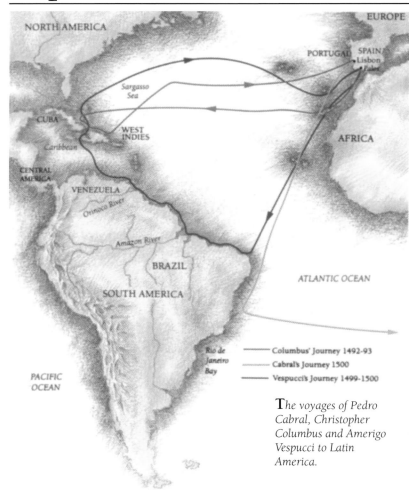

The voyages of Pedro Cabral, Christopher Columbus and Amerigo Vespucci to Latin America.

Columbus' Journey 1492-93
Cabral's Journey 1500
Vespucci's Journey 1499-1500

At the end of the fifteenth century, the lives of the people of Latin America changed forever: the Europeans were about to sail west. They soon arrived, thrust their flags into the ground, and took possession of America.

Christopher Columbus

Christopher Columbus arrived in 1492 sailing under the Spanish flag. His landing almost caused war between Spain and Portugal because both countries claimed rights to "the Indies," as they called this new continent. The Pope intervened and settled the dispute with the Treaty of Tordesillas (1494) which drew a line across the continent from north to south. Lands east of the line belonged to Portugal and lands found to the west belonged to Spain.

A portrait of Christopher Columbus

Exploring for Trade

When Columbus landed in America in 1492, he was looking for a new way to get to the East by sea from Europe. During the Middle Ages (c.fifth-fifteenth centuries), all trade between these two areas had been overland in long **caravans** across Asia to Constantinople. But Constantinople had been taken over by the **Turks** and Europeans were no longer welcome there. European merchants needed new trading routes. The Portuguese explored the African coast in search of a passage to the Indian Ocean. Columbus was convinced that the Earth was not flat, which was what most people believed at the time, but was round. He thought that if he sailed to the west, he would finally reach the East. Columbus had no idea that there was an entire continent in between.

This late sixteenth-century drawing shows Columbus being welcomed by natives of the Americas.

A *Dutch painting of Portuguese fighting ships (called carracks) of c.1530. It was about this time that the Portuguese explored the coast of Brazil.*

Animals and Gods

At first, the Europeans thought that the people of Latin America were ruled by the great and famous Japanese and Chinese emperors. They also thought that the new lands were as wealthy as those that the Venetian trader, Marco Polo (1254-1324), had written about in his famous *Travels of Marco Polo.* Columbus wrote in his diary that he thought he had arrived at "paradise" because the people and the land were so beautiful. But the Europeans soon decided that Indians did not have souls and treated them like animals.

Many Aztec myths were about splendid gods who would come to Earth one day (see page 19). When the Spaniards arrived from the east, on horseback and in shining armor, the Indians were overjoyed. They welcomed the Spaniards with open arms as if they were gods (see page 28).

A Race to Get Rich

Columbus made four voyages to America before he finally explored the mainland of Central America in 1502. Meanwhile, the Portuguese had sailed to India for the first time by going around southern Africa. Spain and Portugal were both determined to expand their empires and the two nations were trying to get as rich as possible as quickly as possible—finding new trading routes and lands became important to their success.

New Maps

Each Spanish expedition explored more land and bit by bit maps were drawn of the unknown continent. At first only the coastline was known to these new explorers. Some of the men who had accompanied Columbus on his voyages made their own expeditions to northern Latin America. At Maracaibo, they found lake villages and called the region Venezuela, which means "small Venice" in Spanish (after the Italian city). Other men traded pearls and wood with the Indians. In 1499, Vicente Yáñez Pinzón (1460-1524), who had accompanied Columbus on his 1492 voyage, crossed the Equator, found the mouth of the Amazon River and arrived in northeast Brazil.

The Portuguese were also exploring and after Pedro Cabral (1460-1526) arrived in Brazil in 1500, they explored the south of Latin America. Two years later they reached Rio de Jañeiro Bay. Portuguese ships sailed home loaded with the precious red wood of the land which was called Brazil—the name finally given to the country by Europeans.

In Search of Another Sea

By the beginning of the sixteenth century it was obvious that this new continent was not Asia as the explorers had first thought. The land was too big to be an island and so the search for a route to the Indies went on. Some explorers ventured inland and the Spaniard Vasco Núñez de Balboa (1475-1519) became the first European to see the Pacific Ocean when he crossed the Isthmus of Panama in 1513. But this was not a suitable trading route for ships and so the search for a **passage** to the Pacific Ocean continued. People explored the Amazon River but were disappointed to find that it was not a route to the sea. Further south, the La Plata Estuary provided no access to the Pacific. Finally, in 1519, the Portuguese voyager Ferdinand Magellan (1480-1521) began his journey of discovery west in one of the most difficult voyages ever made (see box right).

Dividing up Latin America

In 1534 Charles I of Spain and John III of Portugal decided to divide up and **colonize** Latin America. The kings drew straight lines on the map parallel to the Equator. East of the line originally agreed in 1494 in the Spanish town of Tordesillas, the coast of Brazil and the surrounding area was divided into 15 captainships (*capitanias*) and was given to Portuguese noblemen and businessmen. On the Spanish side of the Tordessillas Line (the west, see map opposite), four huge sections—Nueva Castilla, Nueva Toledo, Nueva Andalucia and Nueva Leon—were given to captains to govern.

Around the World

Magellan and his crew lived with the Indians of southern Argentina for a while during their freezing winter. The Indians wore thick fur wound around their feet and the sailors called them *Patagoncs*, which means "big feet." Magellan explored the small rivers, islands and dangerous rocks of the coast helped by the Onas Indians, who lit bonfires along the shore to guide their ships. Because of these bonfires, Magellan called the place Fire Land or Tierra del Fuego.

   Once the passage had finally been discovered, Magellan started a two-month crossing of the Pacific Ocean. Under the blazing sun water became undrinkable, food went rotten and the men were forced to eat rats, sawdust and leather. When they arrived at the islands which are now known as the Philippines, in 1521, Magellan was killed in an attack by the natives. Under the leadership of his lieutenant, Sebastián El Cano (1476-1526), his crew carried on and finally arrived back in Spain later in 1521. After three years of traveling, having survived fire, ice, storms and mutiny they arrived home. They were the first men to sail around the world.

A *portrait of Ferdinand Magellan*

A *sixteenth-century engraving of Vasco Núñez de Balboa.*

This late sixteenth-century engraving shows a popular European view of the cruelty of the Spanish conquest of Peru (see page 29).

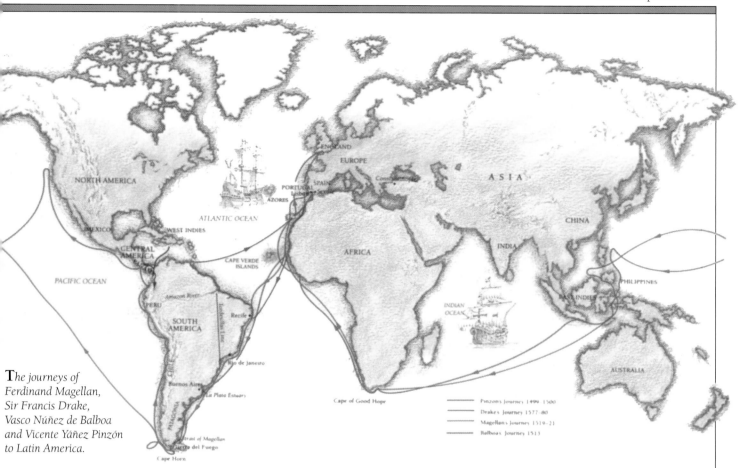

The journeys of Ferdinand Magellan, Sir Francis Drake, Vasco Núñez de Balboa and Vicente Yáñez Pinzón to Latin America.

Pinzons Journey 1499-1500
Drakes Journey 1577-80
Magellans Journey 1519-21
Balboas Journey 1513

God and Gold

In their search for new trading routes by sea, the conquerors had discovered new lands. They found that most of the inhabitants were friendly and worshiped many gods. The new visitors also came with Roman Catholic priests who tried to convert the Indians to Christianity. But many priests, soldiers and sailors came to Latin America in search of gold, silver, pearls, gems and slaves and they were prepared to kill entire communities to get them.

A *portrait of Sir Francis Drake*

Drake the Pirate!

Some years after Magellan's voyage, Elizabeth I of England sent Sir Francis Drake (1545-96) on a voyage around the world. Drake had already attacked Spanish ships and lands in the Caribbean. After reaching the Pacific Ocean, Drake sailed along the coast so that he could raid Spanish colonies in Chile and Peru. Nobody expected his surprise attacks and he captured a great deal of gold.

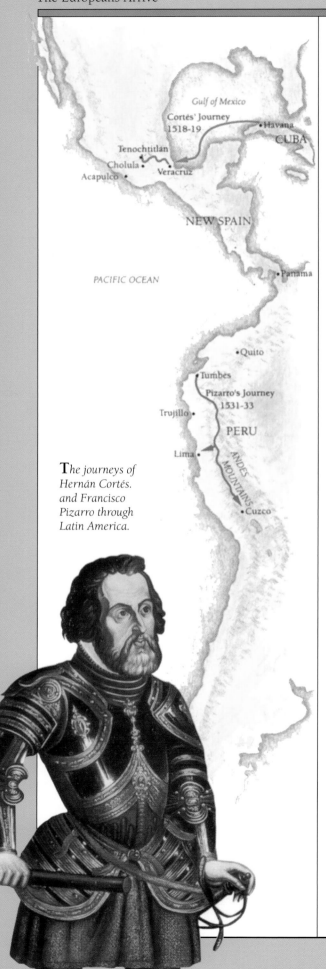

The journeys of Hernán Cortés. and Francisco Pizarro through Latin America.

A nineteenth-century European drawing of Spanish monks destroying Mexican religious statues.

Exploring to Conquer

The Conquest of Mexico

Mexico was conquered from 1519 to 1521 by the Spaniard Hernán Cortés (1485-1547), who arrived with guns, horses and fierce dogs. When he landed with his men, Cortés ordered his ships to be dismantled so that they could not return home. The Aztec emperor, Montezuma, sent Cortés presents—including a golden image of the sun and a silver moon as big as a cartwheel. These offerings made Cortés greedier and more anxious to get to the capital of Tenochtitlán. Cortés made alliances with Montezuma's enemies, destroyed Aztec temples and cities, and erected crosses on the ruins.

Quetzalcoatl was the Aztec god of crossroads and when the Aztecs saw the Spaniard's Christian crosses, they were convinced that the white, bearded men of ancient legend had arrived from the east as gods (see page 19). At the capital, Montezuma welcomed Cortés as if he were the god Quetzalcoatl. When the Spaniards opened fire on a religious procession, the Indians realized their mistake and started fighting. The Spaniards besieged the city for months until the Aztecs were finally defeated.

A portrait of Hernán Cortés by the Master of Saldana (left).

A *European painting of the last battle for Mexico, Cortés is dressed in armor and is waving his sword from the back of his horse in the foreground.*

The Conquest of Peru

The Inca emperor Huayna Capac died shortly before the Spaniards captured Peru. His death was followed by a civil war between his two sons, Huascar (who controlled southern Peru) and Atahualpa (who controlled Ecuador). The Spaniard Francisco Pizarro (1470-1541) arrived in Peru in 1532 to find the country already devastated by civil war. Pizarro had been planning his expedition for a long time because he had heard of the fabulous wealth of the Incas. He brought with him 180 armed men, 37 horses and some interpreters. Pizarro invited Atahualpa to a meeting but when he arrived Pizarro's men killed Atahualpa's soldiers and arrested him.

Buying Freedom

In order to buy his freedom, Atahualpa offered the ransom of a small room filled once with gold and twice with silver. It took the Incas many months to collect this treasure from all the corners of their empire. Even 700 gold plaques from the Temple of the Sun in Cuzco were included. One fifth of the treasure was intended as an offering to the king of Spain and each soldier received a fortune. But Atahualpa did not buy his freedom because Pizarro had him strangled. After Atahualpa's death it was easy for Pizarro to conquer the rest of Peru by the end of 1533.

A *popular eighteenth-century engraving of Francisco Pizarro.*

The *execution of Atahualpa in 1532 as depicted in 1615 by the artist Guaman Poma de Ayala.*

Legendary Treasures

This Pre-Columbian gold mask has eyes of platinum, which are hung from tiny wires. It was treasure like this that the conquistadors were in search of.

Aguirre de Lope (c.1510-1561) joined an expedition of 300 men in Peru to find the treasures of El Dorado in 1560. The party left Lima, crossed the Andes and followed the Huallaga and Marañon rivers. When they reached the Amazon, Aguirre led a mutiny and then took his men down the Amazon raiding villages as he went. Aguirre was captured and executed in 1561.

The fabulous treasures the conquerors took from the Aztecs and the Incas were nothing compared with the legend of El Dorado. After the civilizations which really existed were conquered, the search for mythical golden cities and treasures began in earnest.

The Search for El Dorado

The most enduring Latin American legend was that of El Dorado—the Gold Man. This story probably originated from a Muisca religious ritual. The Muisca Indians (see box on page 12) were part of the Chibcha tribe who lived in the highlands of Colombia near an almost perfectly round lake. Every year the Indians gave a ceremony to thank the golden god that they believed lived at the bottom of the lake. During the ceremony their chief was anointed with a sticky oil and then sprayed with gold dust until he became a glittering, living statue. At the head of a procession, he went to the lake and paddled a raft to the middle of the

This is the lake of Guatavita, Colombia, where Chibcha chiefs inspired the legend of El Dorado.

water, then he dived in and washed away the gold. On the shore, his people threw emeralds and gold objects into the water as offerings to their god.

Another story told of a kingdom in the rain forest where everybody and everything (except food) was covered with gold that was washed off every day. This story became part of the El Dorado legend. Many greedy people looked for El Dorado, leaving destruction in their trail. The Spanish king gave Venezuela to the Germans, who occupied the land and terrorized the natives in their search for gold. They took 220 pounds (100 k) of gold but did not find El Dorado.

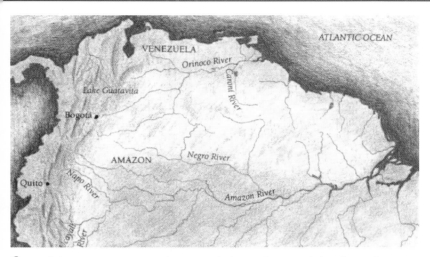

*S*ome of the rivers European explorers traveled up in their search for El Dorado.

The Search Continues

The Englishman Sir Walter Raleigh (c. 1552-1618) traveled up the Orinoco River with five small boats in 1595 in search of El Dorado. Each boat carried 100 men who had to row against the current. When Raleigh's boats finally came out of the delta, they went on to join the main flow of the Orinoco. Raleigh was amazed at the beauty of the landscape and declared, *"we passed the most beautiful country that ever mine eyes beheld."*

Raleigh stopped near the village of Morequito at the mouth of the Caroní River and met the head of the village, a man called Topiawari. Topiawari was supposed to be 110 years old and yet he walked many miles through the forest to bring Raleigh presents of food. Raleigh and his men were unable to get up the Caroní River and so they returned to England taking with them disappointed hopes and more stories of El Dorado.

Pirates!

The French, the English and the Dutch did not want to accept the division of Latin America as decided by the Treaty of Tordesillas (see pages 24 and 26). These nations wanted a share of the treasures found in the new land. Pirates attacked Spanish and Portuguese ships that returned to Europe loaded with Latin American gold and silver. More European expeditions were organized. France established two colonies in Brazil and the Dutch ruled the cities and sugar-cane plantations of the Brazilian northeast for 25 years. But these colonists eventually fled from the Portuguese, who decided to protect their interests.

*A*n *early seventeenth-century picture of Raleigh taking the Spanish governor of St. Joseph (Trinidad) prisoner in 1595.*

5 Exploring New Countries

A Silver Mountain

A *seventeenth-century engraving of the local population mining silver from Potosí.*

Near the village of Potosí in Bolivia, in 1545, an Indian discovered a mountain that glittered with pure silver. In less than 30 years, Potosí had as many inhabitants as contemporary London. One century later, during a religious celebration, the stones that paved the streets of Potosí were replaced by silver bars—they say that even the horseshoes of Potosí were made of silver. Potosí became a wealthy city where many artists worked for churches, rich households and palaces. There was so much silver at Potosí that what was transported to Spain in one and a half centuries was equal to three times the existing European stocks of silver at the time.

Modern-day Potosí and the colonial town that grew up around the mountain.

A Single Ruler

In 1578, King Sebastian of Portugal disappeared during a battle against the Moors, leaving no heir. The Portuguese crown went to Philip II of Spain in 1580 and the two kingdoms remained united for 60 years. During this time nobody worried about the Tordesillas line (see pages 24, 26 and 31). The Portuguese and their Brazilian-born descendants, the Bandeirantes (also known as the "pathfinders"), seized this opportunity to extend their territory and explore deep into the continent.

At first, the Bandeirantes explored inland to find Indian slaves to work the sugar plantations. But Jesuit priests who had built missions in Paraguay defended the Indians. European slave ships transported African slaves to work the fields of northern Brazil so the emphasis of the Bandeirante expeditions changed. They began to look for precious metals and gems instead of slaves.

A *portrait of Philip II of Spain (1527-98).*

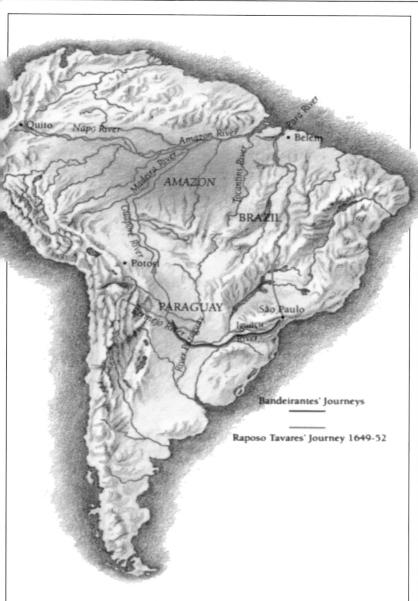

Gold Mines

Until the mid-eighteenth century the Bandeirantes roamed the interior in search of diamonds and gold and new cities were founded. The capital of Brazil changed from Bahia, near the sugar plantations, to Rio de Jañeiro, near the mines. Most of the wealth from these areas traveled to Portugal and then to England which supplied Portugal (and Brazil) with manufactured (factory-made) goods. Part of this wealth paid for more and more African slaves to work in the mines. Part of the money was used by the Roman Catholic Church to build wonderful churches filled with gold, paintings and sculptures. The Portuguese took gold and diamonds from Latin America and did not build the economy up in return. For example, they abandoned road building and made weaving a crime. Their aim was to prevent goods produced in Latin America competing with goods shipped into the continent from Portugal.

The Catholic church built many churches and Catholicism is the main religion of modern-day Latin America.

This map shows the journey of Raposo Tavares and the explorations of the Bandeirantes into the heart of their own country.

Raposo Tavares

Through their explorations, the Bandeirantes wiped out the imaginary line that divided the Portuguese and the Spanish. They left São Paulo (Brazil) and followed the rivers that flowed west. They traveled as far as they could in order to extend the boundaries of their country and search for gold. The most remarkable of these travelers was Raposo Tavares whose expedition on foot took four years and covered 7,500 miles (12,000 km). Tavares traveled through modern-day Paraguay and Bolivia, up the Madeira River to the Amazon, from the Atlantic Ocean to the Andes Mountains and from the Tropic of Capricorn to the Equator.

Coming of Age

Time for Change

Latin America produced gold, silver, emeralds and diamonds which ships carried to Europe along with wood, sugar, tobacco and cotton. Spain and Portugal had a **monopoly** on all trade and they imposed heavy taxes on their colonies.

The Criollos were people with European parents who were born in Latin America. The Criollos wanted a bigger share of government and more power but the slaves and original inhabitants of Latin America did most of the work and owned very little. Gradually people began to demand freedom from colonization.

Meanwhile, in Britain, the **Industrial Revolution** (second half of the eighteenth century) was beginning. This commercial revolution required raw materials to make new products and people to buy the products in order to succeed. But the slaves and poor people of Latin America had no wealth and could not buy anything. International pressure against slavery was growing stronger and stronger.

Pineapples and sweetcorn (maize) came to Europe via Latin America.

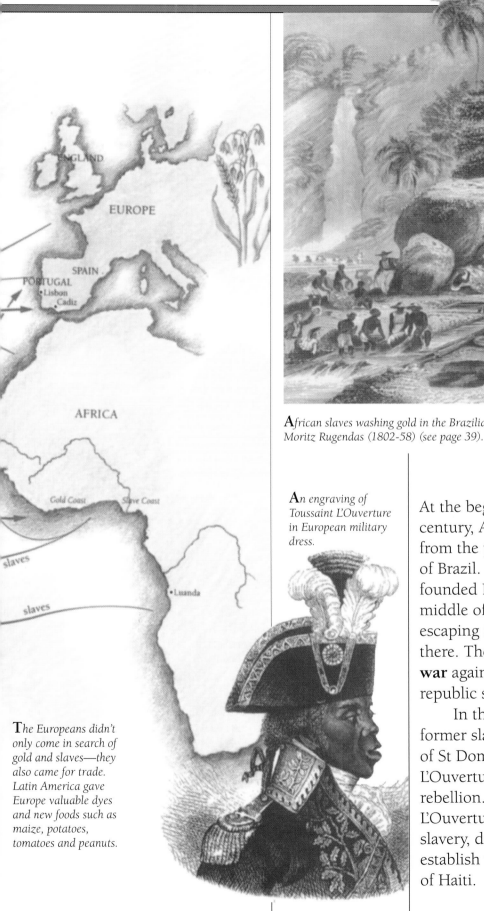

*A*frican slaves washing gold in the Brazilian Highlands. This engraving is by Johann Moritz Rugendas (1802-58) (see page 39).

*A*n engraving of Toussaint L'Ouverture in European military dress.

*T*he Europeans didn't only come in search of gold and slaves—they also came for trade. Latin America gave Europe valuable dyes and new foods such as maize, potatoes, tomatoes and peanuts.

Rebel Republics

At the beginning of the seventeenth century, African slaves began to escape from the plantations in the northeast of Brazil. They explored inland and founded Palmares, a republic in the middle of a forest. Soon, slaves were escaping from every plantation to go there. They fought a fierce **guerrilla war** against the Portuguese and their republic survived for over a century.

In the Caribbean, in 1791, a former slave from the French colony of St Domingue, Toussaint L'Ouverture (1746-1803), led a rebellion. In only eight years, L'Ouverture managed to abolish slavery, defeat the French army and establish the independent Republic of Haiti.

Fighting for Freedom

Brazil made several attempts to gain independence during the eighteenth century. The most significant one was led by Joaquim José de Silva Xavier (1748-92), known as Tiradentes, in 1789. However, many wealthy Brazilians were more interested in keeping slavery. When the country finally became independent in 1822, it did so as a kingdom under the rule of a Portuguese prince. The end of slavery did not come until 1888 and the monarchy survived until 1889, when the republic was established.

Spanish America was divided into provinces and **viceroyalties** by the eighteenth century. The struggle for independence was unsuccessful for a long time. Property owners became involved in the fight for freedom after the collapse of the Spanish monarchy when Napoleon Bonaparte (1769-1821) invaded Spain in 1808.

The year 1810 was very important for freedom in Latin America. In Venezuela, Francisco Miranda (1750-1816) led a war of independence over a period of two years, but was eventually betrayed and imprisoned by the Spaniards. But the battle for Venezuela was eventually won by Simón Bolívar (see box) in 1821.

In 1811, in Mexico, a priest called Miguel Hidalgo (1753-1811) led an armed rebellion against the Spanish. He was defeated and killed but was immediately replaced by another priest, José Morelos (1765-1815), who tried to abolish slavery and establish a republic. Morelos was shot in 1815 and Mexico did not become independent until 1821 when it was ruled by a Mexican army officer and then as a republic (1824).

Simón Bolívar

Simón Bolívar (1783-1830) was known as "the Liberator." Bolívar freed his home of Venezuela in 1821, Colombia and Ecuador in 1822, Peru in 1824 and Bolívia (named after him) in 1825. Bolívar started fighting the Spanish in Venezuela in 1810 but was defeated and had to flee the country. Bolívar was president of Gran Colombia (a union of Venezuela, Colombia and Ecuador) from 1822-30.

A *French engraving of Mexico City showing the cathedral and main square from* Voyage Pittoresque en Mexique (Picturesque Voyage Through Mexico) *of 1836, by Carl Nebel.*

A *map showing some of the major battles San Martin and Bolívar fought to bring independence to Latin America.*

T*his detail of the Mexican* Independence Mural *(1960) by Juan O'Gorman shows Father Hidalgo in the center holding up a flaming torch and Simón Bolívar standing to his right.*

A Unified Nation

After securing the independence of Venezuela, Simón Bolívar went on a campaign to free Colombia and Ecuador. His dream was to unify all the Spanish-speaking countries in one free, rich and powerful state.

During the same period, another general, José de San Martín (1778-1850), came from Spain in 1812 to join a rebellion in Buenos Aires (Argentina) that later led to the independence of Argentina and Paraguay. San Martín crossed the Andes Mountains with Chile's Bernardo O'Higgins at the head of a well prepared army and freed Chile in 1817-18. With ships under the command of Lord Cochrane (a Scottish adventurer), he landed his troops on the Peruvian coast in 1820 and forced the Spaniards to take refuge in the mountains. Two years later, San Martín and Bolívar met and decided that the final attack against Spanish power in America would be made by Bolívar. The Battle of Ayacucho was won by Bolívar's general Antonio José de Sucre (1795-1830), in 1824. Sucre went on to become the first president of Bolivia in 1826.

In less than 15 years of war, most of Latin America was free—except for Cuba and Puerto Rico, which remained colonies until 1898. But Bolívar's dream of a united Latin America did not come true because the differences between regions were too great.

6 Visitors and Travelers

Travelers' Tales

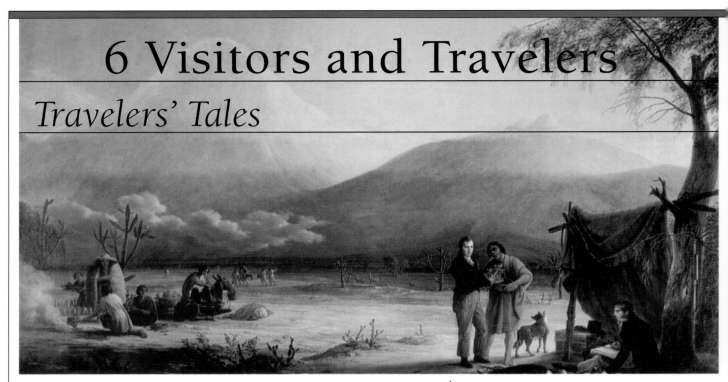

A painting of Humboldt (center right) and Bonpland (bottom right-hand corner) with the mountains of Chimborazo in the background.

Eighteenth-century Scientists Explore

During the eighteenth century geographical and scientific societies sponsored expeditions all over Latin America. In 1735 the French Academy of Sciences sent 11 scientists to take measurements under the line of the Equator. These men eventually proved correct Sir Isaac Newton's theory that the Earth is larger at the Equator. Their calculation of the length of the Equator was the basis for all measurements of length, volume and weight in the metric system.

La Condamine and Ferreira

The leader of the French Academy expedition was Charles Marie de la Condamine (1701-74). La Condamine was a mathematician who was also interested in natural history, astronomy and cartography. La Condamine explored about 2,500 miles (4,000 km) of the Amazon region, examining plants, birds, animals, people and the landscape as he went. On his return to Paris in 1745, La Condamine published accounts of his journeys across the new continent and inspired interest in the exploration of Latin America in scientists, **botanists**, cartographers and artists all over Europe,

It wasn't just European scientists who were investigating Latin America. Alexandre Rodrigues Ferreira (1756-1815) was born in Brazil and trained as a natural historian in Portugal. Ferreira went to Brazil in 1783 to explore the rivers of his homeland and write papers on tribes and their masks, pipes, pottery and huts.

Alexander von Humboldt

The most important scientist to explore Latin America during the colonial period was the German, Alexander von Humboldt (1769-1859). Humboldt spent five years with the French botanist Aimé Bonpland (1773-1858) studying Central America and the Andes. Humboldt wrote 30 books about the highlands, volcanoes, rain forests, geography, politics and economy of Latin America.

A *drawing of a black-headed Cacajao monkey from one of Humboldt and Bonpland's books on the animals of Latin America.*

Nineteenth-century Scientists Explore

Carl Friedrich Philip von Martius (1794-1868) traveled to Brazil in 1818 to investigate tribal Indians and natural history. Martius returned to Europe two years later with a collection of plant specimens and Indian artifacts. The studies Martius made were important in establishing academic writing on Brazilian Indians after this time. His collection of 6,500 plants formed the basis of the *Flora Braziliensis* which was a catalogue of Latin American plants written with the zoologist, Johann Baptist von Spix (1781-1826).

The Frenchman Alcide Orbigny (1802-57) sailed for Rio. Orbigny explored Argentina, Paraguay, Cuba, Venezuela, Colombia and Bolivia. In 1829 he explored Patagonia for nine months, eventually visiting the Tehuelche Indians and going on an ostrich hunt.

The Englishmen Henry Walter Bates (1825-92) and Alfred Russell Wallace (1823-1913) traveled to the Amazon in 1848 to collect anything they could find to further their knowledge of Latin America. Wallace lost his precious specimens and notes at sea, but when Bates returned to England in 1859 he took with him huge collections that included over 3,000 newly discovered species of insect.

The German Karl von den Steinen (1855-1929) was one of the last great explorer-scientists of the nineteenth century. Steinen's two-volume work on the remote Indians of Brazil was of major scientific importance.

An engraving of explorers making their way through the rain forest from Carl Nebel's Voyage Pittoresque en Mexique (Picturesque Voyage Through Mexico) *of 1836.*

A *painting by Debret*

Piecing Together the Puzzle

Most scientific expeditions published accounts of their journeys, relating new discoveries and providing maps. Little by little, European knowledge of rivers, mountains and the entire continent of Latin America became more accurate— it was as if the map of the continent was a jigsaw puzzle and each expedition supplied a new piece of the picture.

Naturalists drew new plants and animals and artists made sketches of entire areas. The Frenchman, Jean-Baptiste Debret (1768-1848), spent 15 years in Brazil painting everything he saw in great detail. On his return to France in 1831, Debret published three volumes of pictures of Latin American life. The German artist, Johann Moritz Rugendas, drew ordinary scenes in Brazil, Mexico, Chile, Peru and Bolivia.

The Race for Knowledge

Colonel Fawcett disappeared while exploring in search of legendary ancient Indian cities deep in the rain forests of Brazil.

Charles Lindbergh (1902-74) flew the Atlantic Ocean in 1927. He later explored Latin America from the air (bottom right) in search of the ruins of lost civilizations.

Lost and Found Cities

In 1909, the Englishman Colonel Percy Fawcett (1867-1925) was hired by the Bolivian government to study a river on the border with Brazil. After this expedition to the Brazilian Highlands, Fawcett saw an eighteenth-century document mentioning a fabulous "lost city," complete with silver mines. In 1920 Fawcett organized an unsuccessful expedition to look for the city. He returned to Brazil in 1925 and explored with his son and a friend, but they all disappeared without trace in the Amazon region.

Other important cities were rediscovered. In Central America important Maya ruins were spotted from an airplane (see page 15). In Peru, the American archaeologist

An explorer's boat being hauled up a waterfall in 1876.

Dr. Hiram Bingham (1875-1919) found the ruins of Machu Picchu near Cuzco (see pages 22-23) in 1911. More recently, the ruins of the Aztec temple destroyed by Cortés were found in the main square of Mexico City (see page 36) when workmen were digging a new underground in the 1980s.

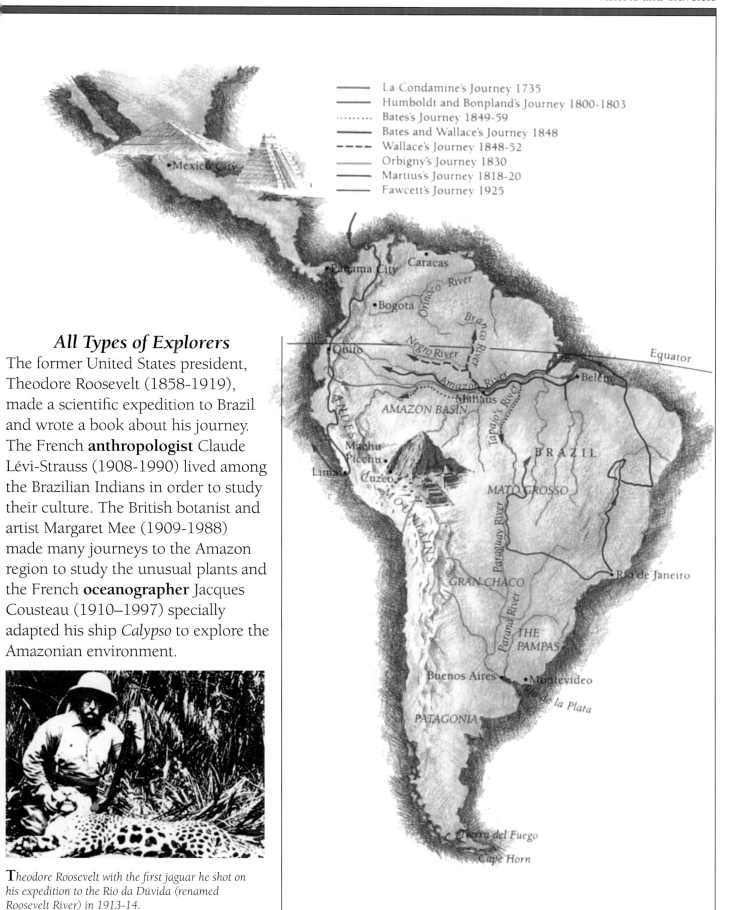

La Condamine's Journey 1735
Humboldt and Bonpland's Journey 1800-1803
Bates's Journey 1849-59
Bates and Wallace's Journey 1848
Wallace's Journey 1848-52
Orbigny's Journey 1830
Martius's Journey 1818-20
Fawcett's Journey 1925

All Types of Explorers

The former United States president, Theodore Roosevelt (1858-1919), made a scientific expedition to Brazil and wrote a book about his journey. The French **anthropologist** Claude Lévi-Strauss (1908-1990) lived among the Brazilian Indians in order to study their culture. The British botanist and artist Margaret Mee (1909-1988) made many journeys to the Amazon region to study the unusual plants and the French **oceanographer** Jacques Cousteau (1910–1997) specially adapted his ship *Calypso* to explore the Amazonian environment.

Theodore Roosevelt with the first jaguar he shot on his expedition to the Rio da Dúvida (renamed Roosevelt River) in 1913-14.

7 Modern Times

Wealth and Poverty

Modern Latin America is made up of 22 independent (no longer colonized) countries. But home government did not instantly bring economic wealth. Former Spanish and Portuguese colonies were still under a great deal of foreign influence long after independence.

Producing Food to Export

The newly independent nations of Latin America were free to trade with countries other than Spain and Portugal. At the time when Europe was dominated by the Industrial Revolution (see page 34) new manufactured goods were sent all around the globe thanks to railways and steamships. The new European products needed large supplies of raw materials and Latin America specialized in supplying some of these materials. The economic growth that followed was based on the production of goods such as copper, sugar, rubber and cotton, for international markets. Agricultural land was planted with crops grown for export rather than those needed for the local people. New local industries were not protected and many collapsed when faced with competition from large and powerful foreign companies.

A newly-built railway bridge crosses a valley in the Andes Mountains (Peru) in the 1870s.

The Panama Canal was built from 1904 to 1914 across Central America. This photograph was taken the day the canal opened.

Railways and Steamships

New technology brought many changes to Latin America. Steamships made mass transportation of goods possible and remote regions were more fully explored. There was no complete network of railways. Most of the railway lines had been built to transport goods for export. Some connected the mines to the ports and others were built where river navigation was difficult. When mass-production of cars began in North America (1908) it became possible to travel through the continent more easily.

A Few Rich People

The wealth produced by this sudden devevelopment was unevenly distributed. The landowners became rich, bought more land, and got richer. The ordinary people had to survive on very low wages and could not afford to own land. The workers couldn't move away to find something better because they were always in debt to the employer's shop which was usually the only one in the area.

The prices of the raw materials Latin America sold dropped lower and lower, while the prices of things produced by Europe got higher and higher. The countries outside Latin America were still richer and still controlled the Latin American economy to a certain extent.

The International Debt

International banks opened branches in Latin America to safeguard their investments in cattle, **nitrates**, copper, rubber, sugar, coffee, cotton and other products. Money was lent to Latin American governments by foreign governments for investment in railways, ports, roads, water and sewage systems, gas, electric power and, later, telephones. Most public services (like railways) were owned by foreign companies. The massive interest payments on foreign government loans are still being paid off by Latin America today.

Cândido Rondon (1865-1958)

The Brazilian, Cândido Rondon, served in the army throughout his long life. When he died he was known as "the Marshall of Peace." He traveled through the wilderness for 40 years, mostly on foot, on horseback and in canoes, covering nearly 24,000 miles (40,000 km), which is the circumference of the Earth itself. Rondon erected telegraph lines through the jungle, inspected frontiers, explored unknown territory throughout Brazil and made contact with many isolated Indian tribes. Even when attacked, his troops always followed his command to *"Die, if necessary. But never kill."* Rondon ran the Indian Protection Service from 1910 until his death in 1958. Through this agency he championed the rights of native Latin American Indians.

A young boy earns his living as a street trader in Lima, Peru.

Despite the transport revolution of the last 100 years, traditional types of travel are still essential, such as this donkey used to collect crops in Mexico.

Latin America Today

The mixture of rich and poor housing in the city of Rio de Janeiro, Brazil.

Traditional cultures have survived even in areas known to Europeans for 500 years—a Cuna native girl from Panama.

Conflicts

Despite the millions of immigrants from Europe and Asia bringing labor and new skills to Latin America, progress in the area was held back by internal conflicts. These took many forms but were usually a result of the great gap between rich and poor, despite the continent's natural wealth in land and minerals.

During the 1960s and 1970s the military seized power in many countries, leading to the imprisonment, torture and killing of those who opposed them. Civil war in Guatemala from 1960 to 1996 killed over 200,000. El Salvador's civil war in the 1980s killed 70,000 and resulted in 2 billion dollars worth of damage.

In Brazil and Mexico landless peasants have risen in armed revolt. In Peru, Bolivia and Colombia peasant poverty has encouraged large-scale production of drugs, leading to huge profits for criminal gangs. In most major cities poverty has led to violent crime and kidnapping; Politicians tackling these problems have sometimes failed.

Natural disasters have also taken their toll—earthquakes in Guatemala in 1976, in Mexico in 1985 and in El Salvador in 2001, and Hurricane Mitch devastated El Salvador, Honduras and Nicaragua in 1998. Floods ravaged Brazil in 2011. These events killed thousands and left millions homeless.

Latin America remains a diverse land blessed with natural beauty and resources but still battling the conflicts caused by competing forces inside many nations.

A Kayapó Indian uses a video camera to inform people about his culture.

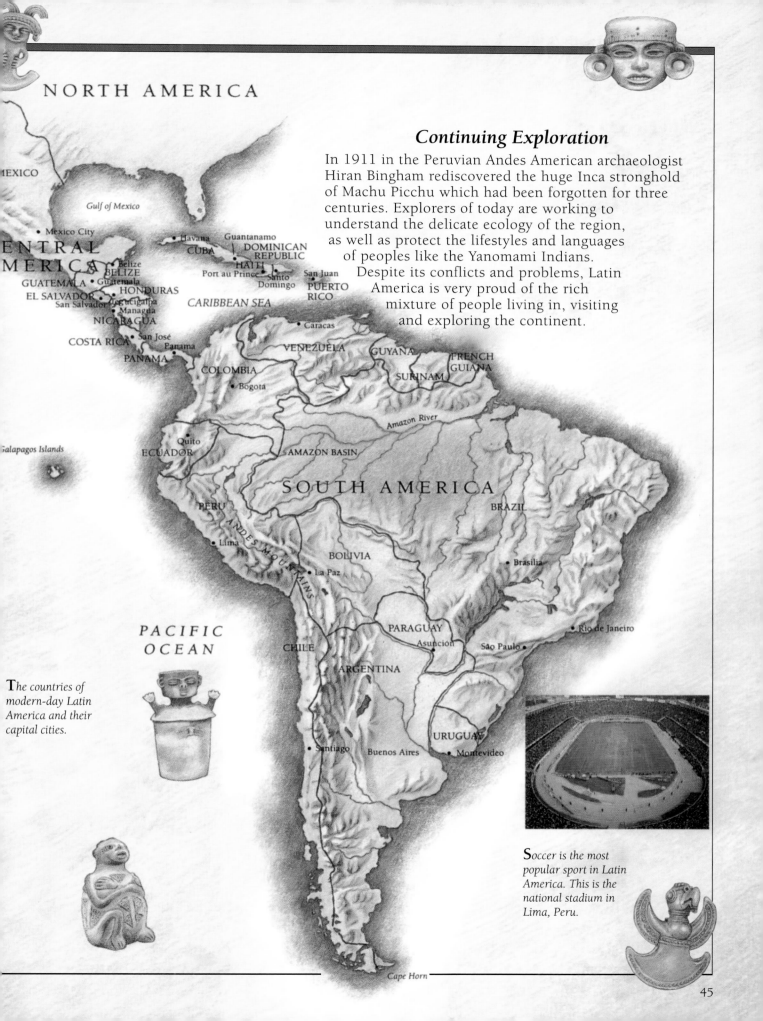

NORTH AMERICA

MEXICO

Gulf of Mexico

• Mexico City

CENTRAL AMERICA

• Havana   Guantanamo
CUBA   DOMINICAN
REPUBLIC
• Belize   HAITI
BELIZE   Port au Prince   Santo   San Juan
GUATEMALA   Domingo   PUERTO
• Guatemala   RICO
EL SALVADOR   HONDURAS
San Salvador   Tegucigalpa
• Managua   *CARIBBEAN SEA*
NICARAGUA

COSTA RICA   • San José
• Panama
PANAMA

Galapagos Islands

Continuing Exploration

In 1911 in the Peruvian Andes American archaeologist Hiran Bingham rediscovered the huge Inca stronghold of Machu Picchu which had been forgotten for three centuries. Explorers of today are working to understand the delicate ecology of the region, as well as protect the lifestyles and languages of peoples like the Yanomami Indians. Despite its conflicts and problems, Latin America is very proud of the rich mixture of people living in, visiting and exploring the continent.

• Caracas

VENEZUELA   GUYANA   FRENCH
GUIANA
SURINAM
COLOMBIA
• Bogota

Amazon River

Quito
ECUADOR   • AMAZON BASIN

SOUTH AMERICA

PERU   BRAZIL

• Lima
ANDES MOUNTAINS   BOLIVIA   • Brasília
• La Paz

PACIFIC OCEAN

PARAGUAY   • Rio de Janeiro
Asunción   São Paulo
CHILE

ARGENTINA

The countries of modern-day Latin America and their capital cities.

URUGUAY
• Santiago   Buenos Aires   • Montevideo

Soccer is the most popular sport in Latin America. This is the national stadium in Lima, Peru.

Cape Horn

Latin America Timeline

c.6600 bce	Evidence of maize and squash being farmed in Ecuador.
c.5000	Farming begins in Mexico.
c.2000	Farming throughout Latin America.
c.1200-300	The Chorrera culture (Andes).
c.1200-400	The Olmec culture (Mexico).
c.1200-200	The Chavin culture (Peru).
c.600-200	The Paracas culture (Peru).
c. 1-600 ce	The city of Teotihuaeán is built.
c. 1-700	The Moche civilization.
c.300-900	The Mayan civilization.
900-1200	The Toltec and Chichimec peoples found the city of Tula.
c.1100-1530	The Incas found the city of Cuzco and begin to build their empire.
c. 1345-1530	The Aztec civilization.
1492	Christopher Columbus arrives in Latin America.
1494	The Treaty of Tordesillas is signed.
1519	Magellan sails around the world.
1519-21	The Conquest of Mexico by Cortés.
1532-33	The conquest of Peru by Pizarro.
c.l660-1750s	The Bandeirantes explore Brazil.
1791-99	Toussaint L'Ouverture leads a rebellion of Negro slaves
1810-12	Francisco Miranda leads an unsuccessful war of independence in Venezuela.
1817-18	San Martin liberates Chile.
1821-22	Mexico, Venezuela, Colombia, Ecuador and Brazil become independent.
1898	Cuba and Puerto Rico become independent.
1904-14	Building of the Panama Canal.
1932-35	Paraguay and Bolivia fight over the Chaco region.
1962	The Cuban missile crisis takes place between President Kennedy and Russia's Krushchev.
1970s	Many Latin American countries are ruled by military dictatorships.
1980s	Peru, Argentina. Brazil and Chile hold democratic elections
1992	Earth Summit held in Rio de Janeiro.
1999	Panama regains control of Panama Canal from USA.
2001-2002	Economic crisis in Argentina and Venezuela.
2002	Brazil wins soccer World Cup for fifth time.
1999	Leftist leader Hugo Chavez wins election in Venezuela, which he leads until his death in 2013.
2010	The world watches as Chilean authorities race to rescue 33 miners trapped in a cave-in; all the men are rescued.
2011	Terrible floods kill thousands in Brazil.
2013	Argentina Catholic cardinal Jorge Bergoglio becomes Pope Francis I, the first pope from Latin America.
2014	Soccer's World Cup is played throughout Brazil, attracting visitors and more than a billion TV viewers.
2015	President Obama begins to normalize US-Cuba relations for the first time since the Castro revolution in 1959.
2016	The Summer Olympics were held in Rio de Janiero.

Glossary

A

alpaca: a small animal (about a yard tall) that is related to the camel family and looks like a goat. The alpaca is valued for its hairy coat which can be made into very fine wool.

anthropologist: someone who studies human beings and their cultures.

aqueduct: a man-made channel for water.

archaeologist: someone who studies the past by searching for and examining objects from the past.

artifact: an ancient object.

B

botanist: someone who studies plants.

C

caravans: a group of merchants traveling across land to sell their goods (usually carried by horses, camels or donkeys).

civil war: war between people of the same country.

colonize: when a group of people from one country settle in another land, they colonize it. Sometimes these people take over the new land by force and claim it. This is called colonization.

E

estuary: the name given to the place where a river joins the sea. Estuaries contain a mixture of both fresh and salt water and have tides.

equation: a mathematical formula.

Equator: an imaginary line which circles the Earth at an equal distance from both the North and South Poles.

evaporate: to change a liquid into a vapor by using heat or moving air.

F

fertile: soil that allows plants to grow in it very easily because it is moist and full of minerals for the plants to feed on.

fluvial basin: land carved into the shape of a large basin by the movement of a river.

G

geological: relating to the science of geology. Geology is the study of the structure and history of the Earth.

guerrilla war: a war fought by soldiers who do not belong to an official, national army. Guerrillas use different fighting tactics from official armies, usually involving ambushes and sabotage.

I

Industrial Revolution: a period of social and economic change beginning in Britain in the 1760s. It involved the change from people producing goods at home to working in large factories with newly-invented large machines.

irrigation: to water land and crops with a system of **aqueducts** or small canals.

J

Jesuit: a member of the Roman Catholic Order of Jesus, founded by St. Ignatius in the sixteenth century. The Jesuits traveled all over the world working as missionaries.

M

manioc: a plant **native** to Latin America that is grown for its roots. The roots are ground down and used to make bread and tapioca.

military coup: when the army of a country takes over its government by force this is called a military coup.

monopoly: when one particular country or company dominates a market, service or product it is said to have a monopoly. When this situation occurs the company who hold the monopoly can dictate the price of the product or service.

N

native: a person, plant or animal that belongs to a certain place.

nitrates: are chemicals used in explosives and fertilizers.

O

oceanographer: someone who studies the plants, animals and environments of the world's oceans.

P

Pampas: the name of the flat area of land in Argentina between the Andes Mountains and the Atlantic Ocean.

passage: the name given to a trading route during the fifteenth and sixteenth centuries.

pilgrimage: a journey made by a follower of a religion to a place of special religious significance.

prehistoric: something from a time before history as we know it began. Dinosaurs are prehistoric animals.

Q

Quimbaya: a community of Indians who lived in the central mountain range of Colombia. The Quimbaya made large and intricate objects out of gold such as helmets, masks and crocodile pendants.

R

republic: an independent country which has no monarch and is ruled by an elected government.

S

Sinu: a culture that existed in what is now modern-day Colombia during the fourteenth century. They lived by gathering food and fishing in the Magdalena River valleys. The Sinu were very skilled in the art of casting and hammering gold ornaments.

T

Tairona: the dominant civilization of northeastern Colombia from 1000 CE up to the fourteenth and fifteenth centuries. The Tairona were the finest goldsmiths of the area and built stone houses and roads.

textile: any material woven from spun threads, such as wool and cotton.

Tolima: the Tolima people lived in the middle of the Magdalena Valley in northern Colombia. They were excellent goldsmiths.

tropical: the climate of the area of the Earth between the Tropic of Cancer and the Tropic of Capricorn. These are two imaginary lines the same distance north and south of the **Equator**. The tropical areas of the world are usually very hot and the land is very **fertile**.

Turks: people from Turkey (in southern Europe, next to Greece).

V

viceroyalties: places governed by viceroys, people appointed by a monarch to rule a colony.

Y

yam: a tropical plant, the root of which is eaten like a vegetable.

Index

Photographic credits

Cover: Main: Sfmthd/Dreamstime; disk: mud and dark/Flickr; frog: Dirk Ercken/Dreamstime.
Interior: Ancient Art & Architecture Collection 11, 12 bottom left, 17 bottom left, 22 top left; Andes Press Agency 42 top; Bridgeman Art Library 32 bottom right; Sue Cunningham Photographic 33, 43, bottom, 44 right;John Curtis 10; Dagli Orti 16 bottom, 18 bottom, 24 top, 39 top; E.T. Archive 9 bottom, 19 top right and middle, 29 lop, 36 top; Mary Evans Picture Library 2,26 top, 29 middle, 35 bottom, 40 top right; Dr Kurt Stavenhagen collection, 16 top right Dallas Museum of Art; Giraudon/Bridgeman Art Library 28 bottom; Robert Harding Picture Library 6, 9 top right, 12 bottom right, 17 bottom right, 18 top, 19 top left and bottom British Museum, 25 National Maritime Museum, 26 bottom, 27 National Martime Museum, 36 bottom British Museum, 37, 38 top Schloss Tegel. Berlin and bottom; Hulton Deutsch 16 top left, 24 bottom, 28 lop, 31, 40 bottom; Mansell Collection 5, 26/27, 32 top, 35 top; Andrew Oliver 22 top right, 23 bottom, 43 middle, 45; Royal Geographical Society 3, 7 top and middle right, 8, 9 top left, 39 bottom, 44 left; Nick Saunders/Barbara Heller 14 left; South American Pictures title page, 7 left and bottom right,12 top, 14 right, 15, 17 top, 21, 22 bottom, 23 top, 29 bottom, 30, 32 bottom left, 40 top left, 41, 42 bottom, 43 top, 44 top, Dreamstime: Leon Rafael 13C, Madrugaverde 13T.

6/9/16